BEING
LED
BY THE
SPIRIT

BEING LED BY THE SPIRIT

GREG GLASSFORD

Whitaker House

Unless otherwise indicated, all Scripture quotations are taken from the *King James Version* (KJV) of the Bible.

BEING LED BY THE SPIRIT

Youth Force International
P.O. Box 203
Broken Arrow, OK 74013

ISBN: 0-88368-474-8
Printed in the United States of America
Copyright © 1989 by Greg Glassford

Whitaker House
580 Pittsburgh Street
Springdale, PA 15144

2 3 4 5 6 7 8 9 10 11 12 13 / 06 05 04 03 02 01 00 99 98 97 96

Contents

Foreword

The greatest struggle that any believer will ever face is the battle that he wages with his flesh. The devil flees when we resist him with the Word of God, but the flesh is ever with us, requiring constant discipline and domination by the new man in Christ. Too many Christian young people are ignorant of the realities of this struggle and therefore succumb to the lust of the flesh. Because he does not understand his own flesh, many a Christian teenager has unnecessarily fallen prey to Satan's devices.

I am pleased that Greg Glassford has addressed this very important subject in such an open and forthright manner. Teenagers need straight talk and real answers from God's Word in the struggles they encounter. And as we have seen during the past few years, these struggles can be a matter of life and death.

Greg is immensely qualified to present this outstanding teaching for young people. He has proven his ministry with faithful service to teens for more than a decade. The fruit of his ministry speaks for itself.

Youth leader, young person, or concerned parent — listen closely to what Greg has to say.

Willie George
Pastor, Church on the Move
Tulsa, Oklahoma

Introduction

No doubt every Christian high school student has faced or has been involved with areas of *the flesh*. As a matter of fact, every Christian is troubled with the hassles of the flesh from time to time.

The level of victory and freedom you enjoy during your stay here on good old planet earth will greatly depend upon how daring you are to apply what God has spoken to help you overcome the many "flesh traps" awaiting you throughout your life.

Because this is true, it is important for us to get more acquainted with the term *the flesh* so that we will not become a victim of its snare.

This book has been written with you, the teenager living in turbulent times, in mind. So be honest with yourself as you flip through these pages. Truth brings freedom. Be honest with God also. Do not attempt to hide something you know is there. As you let honesty and truth prevail, I think you will be surprised at the level of release it will bring in your life.

God believes in you. He wants His absolute best for you. And He knows what weapons have been formed against you. Dive in head first with total dependency on Him and His ability to put you over the top, and watch Him work in you and through you. His Spirit in your spirit are an unbeatable force against the flesh! *"Hey flesh, move over! This is the Spirit talkin' to you!"*

1
What Is "The Flesh" Anyway?

After you were saved, did you ever notice:

- Old habits sneaking up on you?

- Condemnation, guilt and shame flooding your mind because you gave in to one of those habits?

- Attitudes arise that you didn't know were even in you?

- Areas in your life that you just haven't been able to conquer and overcome?

These, and many more, are all indications of *the flesh*.

The flesh is any part of our unregenerated mind or body which has not yet been submitted to Christ and renewed by His Word.

The flesh is an emotional and spiritual force which is often triggered in our lives through areas we have held on to and have not yet given over to the Lord such as bad habits, thought patterns, attitudes, and so forth.

Sooner or later these things will lead to hurt, bondage, and sin (some are already sin), if we allow them to continue.

The flesh is any part of our human nature which is deprived of the Spirit of God and dominated by the appetites of the unrenewed mind.

The Bible says:

> But when you follow your own wrong inclinations your lives will produce these evil results: impure thoughts, eagerness for lustful pleasure, idolatry, spiritism (that is, encouraging the activity of demons), hatred and fighting, jealousy and anger, constant effort to get the best for yourself, complaints and criticisms, the feeling that everyone else is wrong except those in your own little group —

and there will be wrong doctrine, envy, murder, drunkenness, wild parties, and all that sort of thing.

Let me tell you again as I have before, that anyone living that sort of life will not inherit the kingdom of God.

Galatians 5:19-21 TLB

2

Faces of the Flesh

In the Scripture verses we just read, many different *faces of the flesh* are mentioned. Some may sound familiar to you. The *King James Version* of the Bible calls them *works of the flesh* (v. 19).

Each one of these *works* or *faces* of the flesh have different expressions. Let's take a deeper look.

Immorality

Immorality pertains to everything from adultery, homosexuality, pornography, pre-marital sex, and every other sex-related sin. (*Fornication* is used in other translations).

Impurity

Impurity implies an eagerness for lustful pleasure, impure and indecent thoughts. "Impure" denotes *not pure* — mixed so as to lack purity and character, deluded.

Sensuality

Appealing to the senses. Sensuality implies a strong appeal of things which are pleasing to the eyes, ears, touch, etc. It is accompanied by a drive to gratify these desires. (Col. 3:5,6.)

Idolatry

Excessive devotion to, or worship of some person or thing over and above one's own devotion and worship of the Lord God. (Ex. 20:3.)

Sorcery

Spiritism. Encouraging the activity of demons or participating in forbidden practices. (Deut. 18:10-12; Rev. 21:8.)

Enmity/Strife

Strong hatred, hostility, jealous competition, discord, etc. (2 Cor. 12:20.)

Jealousy

Resentful suspicion of a rival. (Prov. 6:34; Ps. 79:5.)

Outbursts of Anger

Constant effort to get your own way by throwing tantrums. (James 1:19,20.)

Dissensions

Constantly arguing, complaining and/or criticizing others which ends in division. (Prov. 6:16-19.)

Factions

Heresy, which is teaching contrary to the Bible or teaching doctrine which is scripturally inaccurate and totally out of context.

Envying

A feeling of ill will because of another's advantages, possessions, etc. Resentful dislike of another who has something that you strongly desire.

Drunkenness and Carousing

Partaking in and supporting wild parties, devious schemes, and troublemaking. Indulging excessively in alcohol, illegal drugs, or any other substance which invades the physical body to do

it harm and/or cause it to react abnormally. (Eph. 5:18; 1 Cor. 6:19,20; Prov. 6:16-19.)

Weapons Formed Against You

These *faces of the flesh* give us a broader scope to better understand what the flesh actually is. Galatians 5:21 NAS states, **...and things like these...**, which tells us that the works of the flesh go far beyond the things mentioned in the above faces list.

As a young man or woman of God, you will eventually discover many weapons which have been formed against your life. Their purpose is to hold you back from fulfilling your potential and attempt to stop you from becoming the champion and mighty warrior God has called you to be. The flesh is one of those arch enemies.

However the Bible promises that **No weapon that is formed against you shall prosper** (Is. 54:17 NAS).

With this in mind, we can approach the trials and temptations of the flesh with a different attitude. There is a way to overcome! Hang in there, we're just getting started.

3
Facades and Facts About the Flesh

There are many misconceptions or "facades" about this thing called the flesh.

A "facade" is the front part of anything with implications of an imposing appearance concealing something inferior.

That's Mr. Webster for you — always giving those easy-to-understand definitions.

Basically, a facade looks like something real, genuine and true on the surface. But as you begin to check it out and take a closer look, you come to realize that it isn't as real, genuine and true as it appears.

As we continue to learn what the flesh is, let's explore a few of the "facades" we've heard and uncover the facts, based upon the Word of God.

FACADE #1:

The moment you are born again, all areas of fleshly bondage instantly disappear.

FACT:

Romans 7:14-20 NAS

> For we know that the law is spiritual; but I am of the flesh, sold into bondage to sin.

> For that which I am doing, I do not understand; for I am not practicing what I would like to do, but I am doing the very thing I hate. But if I do the very thing I do not wish to do, I agree with the Law confessing that it is good.

> So now, no longer am I the one doing it, but sin which indwells me.

> For I know that nothing good dwells in me, that is, in my flesh; for the wishing is present in me, but the doing of the good is not.

> For the good that I wish, I do not do; but I practice the very evil that I do not wish.
>
> But if I am doing the very thing that I do not wish, I am no longer the one doing it, but sin which dwells in me.

Every Christian, at one time or another, has experienced what the Apostle Paul has just described: wishing, desiring, and wanting to do good, but practicing some form of fleshly sin — even in the midst of righteous desire.

In most cases when someone is saved, there are many *immediate* changes which take place in character, personality, and habits.

These changes come as a result of the *new nature of life* which has replaced the *old nature of death*, darkness, and sin.

> Therefore, if any man be in Christ, he is a new creature: old things are passed away; behold, all things are become new.
> **2 Corinthians 5: 17**

This is referring to the inward man, or the new self, the spirit man.

However, *all* areas of past fleshly bondage do not instantly disappear.

The Apostle Paul said that he had to keep his body under subjection all the time. He had to make it his slave. (See 1 Cor. 9:27.)

The implication here is that Paul's body was constantly wanting to fulfill fleshly desires, but he would not allow it!

> But I see a different law in the members of my body, waging war against the law of my mind, and making me a prisoner of the law of sin which is in my members. So then, on the one hand I myself with my mind am serving the law of God, but on the other, with my flesh, the law of sin.
>
> **Romans 7:23-25 NAS**

> For the flesh sets its desire against the Spirit, and the spirit against the flesh; for these are in opposition to one another, so that you may not do the things that you please.
>
> **Galatians 5:17 NAS**

As you can see, there is a constant battle going on between the new you (your spirit), and the flesh. The new you wants to change and conform to the image of Christ, but the flesh doesn't want to cooperate. The flesh wants to keep things the way they were.

If you had an old car and put a new engine in it, what would you have? You'd have an old car with a new engine. From the outside you cannot tell there is a new engine. The rust and dents are still in the old body. It's going to take some work to get the outside of the car looking good as new again.

In the same way, when we are born again, a change takes place. We, in a manner of speaking, get a new engine. But there are still some dents and rust in the old body. It's going to take discipline and hard work, by applying the Word of God, to get those tougher dents out. But you can do it! (We'll discuss how to find the *Escape Hatch* in Chapter 6).

26

FACADE #2:

Satan is the only one to blame for all fleshly bondage in our lives.

FACT:

James 1:14 NAS

> But each one is tempted when he is carried away and enticed by his own lust.

Sometimes we give the devil too much credit by blaming all of life's misfortunes on him. Yes, Satan is the thief who comes to steal, kill, and destroy (John 10:10), but the beginning of fleshly bondage, according to the Word of God, starts through *our own lust!* It comes through those same areas which have not yet been submitted to the Spirit of God.

For example, let's say you've always enjoyed cutting humor or humor at the expense of others, jokes that cut people down. All of a sudden, an opportunity arises to slam one of your friends. You have a choice to make: either you will cast down that thought (knowing the thing you are considering is not Christlike), or you will follow through with the cut-down simply because you cannot resist the response you will get from your other friends. In other words, you know they'll laugh and you like that kind of acceptance. The devil didn't necessarily put you up to that. It was your flesh. It was that area you still enjoy. Therefore, you have not nailed it to the cross, and it still is in full operation in your life.

There are other areas that you may still enjoy: being disobedient to your parents, smoking that first couple of cigarettes, taking those first few drinks or tokes on a joint, lying and stealing. These things start because of our own desire to try it because we think it might be fun. C'mon, admit it. Some of these things were fun at first.

But if we do not put our bodies under subjection and say, "No!" the devil will show up on our doorstep to bring further bondage. Your adversary, the devil, prowls about like a roaring lion, seeking someone to devour. (1 Pet. 5:8 NAS.)

Satan *cannot* enter any part of our lives unless he is invited in, unless the door is open. He is seeking an open door. He is looking for someone who has begun tampering with sin because of their own lust, and cannot find a way out. It is at this point that real bondage enters the scene.

More on this later.

FACADE #3:

After salvation, man still has two natures:

1. Lower nature (the flesh or carnal part)

2. Higher nature (the spirit or eternal part)

FACTS:

After we are born again, we still have trouble with the flesh, but we don't have trouble with the real man — the spirit.

Some people say, "You have to die out to the old self, the old nature." However, when we are born again the *old nature dies* and we have a *new nature in its place.* What we need to do is *die out to the flesh.*

"You mean the old nature and the flesh are not the same thing?" someone may ask.

That is exactly what I mean.

Let's recall our definition of the flesh: "The flesh is any part of our unregenerated mind or body which has not yet been submitted to Christ and renewed by His Word."

Don't let this be confusing.

Your flesh is the same body, the same flesh it was before you were saved accompanied by the same old thoughts.

But the man on the inside which was the old self has become a new self — *a new creature in Christ.* The inward man has become a new man. When this happens then, **...old things are passed**

away; behold, all things are become new (2 Cor. 5:17).

There is a very fine line which divides the old nature and the flesh.

Before you were saved they operated together, hand in hand. But now that you're saved, you have a *new boss* who is starting to lay out a new set of standards.

This new boss is your spirit (the new man, the inward man who is now born again, who used to be the old boss). The flesh used to follow the commands of that old boss, but now the flesh must follow the commands of the new boss. The flesh doesn't like this new order and will rebel at every opportunity to get its own way, so it can operate like it did before the new boss showed up. *Are you still with me?*

A Clearer Picture

We can see this a bit clearer by looking at what happens at a large corporation or business when a new boss arrives on the scene.

Let's imagine for a moment that the Board of Directors of a large corporation just fired the Executive Director because he wasn't getting the job done effectively. So, in place of the old boss, they hire a new Executive Director with the hope that he will get the corporation moving and grooving.

With new leadership comes new rules, guidelines, and standards. An entirely new mode of operation is usually initiated. As a result, many immediate changes are made as the other directors and employees are made aware of the new direction and begin adapting and conforming to the new order.

But, nine times out of ten, there will always be a handful of employees who rebel. They do not want to change. They were comfortable doing things the old way. This type of person is usually given a few weeks to change his mind, adapt, and begin going with the new flow. But if after a few weeks, there is still a rebellious/half-hearted attitude prevailing, that person is history, gone, archives! The new Executive Director realizes that this kind of employee will only hinder progress, and if allowed to stay, will slowly poison other employees with that same rebellious spirit. So in the long run, it is better to get rid of him now!

In the same way, the flesh is like those rebellious employees. Although the old boss is gone forever, the effect he had upon the employees who are still at the firm is still very obvious. Although the *old man died in Christ when you were saved, the effect he had upon your members who are still around is obvious.*

The flesh does not want to change! It wants to keep things the way they were before — it was comfortable there. So the flesh is going to fight the new order. When the spirit shouts, *"Yes!"* the flesh will shout *"No!"*

Just because we face a little resistance is no reason for us to quit! Remember what Paul said? He said, "I buffet my body and *make it my slave."*

He said, "...and *make it* my slave." He didn't ask his flesh, "Excuse me, Mr. Flesh, would you mind if you could be my slave and do what I ask of you without rebelling? Please? Pretty Please?"

No way! Paul knew he (his spirit) was now the boss and that the flesh had to bow down. He demanded it to conform to the new order!

You must also command your flesh! You must also *make it your slave!* No questions asked — end of debate!

Do not let those old, failing ways continue to operate within your new life! You've got to get tough!

Imagine, for a moment, if this Mr. Newboss took over the corporation, but was just as much of a wimp as the old boss. Now if Mr. Newboss is wimpy and does not begin giving the *bold directives* necessary to save the company, immediately the other employees will see that and will begin to run over him, continuing in their old ways. Thus, nothing will change, but even a greater frustration will arise endangering the corporation even more. Although they know they have a new boss, they will not follow his orders — they do not respect him because of his cowardice. Therefore, things continue as they were, as if Mr. Newboss wasn't even there! What a tragedy!

Although a new boss has arrived on the scene inwardly, things will not change outwardly, and the production will continue to drop until Mr. Newboss gets with the program.

Are you a Christian wimp or warrior?

Are you demanding the flesh to line up?

Or are you backing down from a little resistance?

If you are backing off, then the flesh is not lining up with the *New Creation Order.* The flesh is running over you as if there were no Mr. Newboss at all. You can change it! **...greater is he** that is in you, than he that is in the world (1 John 4:4).

So, concluding the *Facts* regarding *FACADE #3*, the *old man is dead* (2 Cor. 5:17; Rom. 6:1-7), the *flesh is still going around* (Gal. 5:17; Rom. 7:23,24) and must be dealt with.

4
Flesh Traps

Now flee from youthful lusts, and pursue righteousness, faith, love and peace, with those who call on the Lord from a pure heart.

2 Timothy 2:22 NAS

In the mountains you will find men who trap various animals for their meat and pelts.

This is their living. They are called "trappers." They will tell you that different traps are required to snare different animals. There are smaller traps for smaller animals, bigger traps for larger animals. Different techniques are also required for different species, because they all have unique instincts, habits, and weak spots.

A good trapper knows his prey. He knows what they like to eat, where

they like to feed, and what time of day they are out in the open, etc.

People are also unique. We all have different weak spots. Teenagers seem to be an easy catch for the flesh and the devil because they are so vulnerable or open to attack. They lack experience and are quick to *boldly go where no man has gone before.*

There are many *flesh traps* that are unique for teens that I want to bring to your attention so that you will gain more insight as to how to avoid these traps in the future.

Paul warned Timothy to *flee youthful lusts.* He called them *"youthful* lusts," or lusts that are especially attractive to the young. Why is this?

You, as a teenager, exemplify energy, vision, and zeal. You are thrilled by adventure, amazed at the supernatural, and intrigued by the forbidden. You love adventure and enjoy experimentation and exploration! There is a sense about many of you that thrives on exploring the unknown or the unexperienced. I believe, for these reasons, your generation has become a primary target for the enemy of your souls.

Hundreds of thousands of teenagers each year find themselves entrapped by numerous temptations, which have now become lifestyles, and they never dreamed it would get so out of hand.

The following *flesh traps* are some of the most popular ones that deceive and trap many.

FLESH TRAP #1: The Media

Television

How easy it is to find yourself sitting in front of the tube for two, three, four, and even over five hours at a time without a bathroom break. It still amazes me how such a small, innocent box can mesmerize millions! By the time of high school graduation, most children will have spent only 11,000 hours in school, but more than 15,000 hours in front of the television.

What are we absorbing during those 15,000 hours? Sensuality, fornication, violence, the occult (in both cute, humorous ways as well as blatant), humanism, and pornography.

Do not be deceived: *"bad company corrupts good morals"* (1 Corinthians 15:33 NAS).

Movies

How popular it has become to have seen the latest "R-Rated" movie!

"What's wrong with that, Greg? Doesn't 'R' mean that it is a *'real good'* movie? Ha, Ha. 'PG' is only *'pretty good,'* but 'X' is *'extra good.'"* That's how some proverbial minds think.

If you are an avid television and movie viewer, the chances are that you have become desensitized to the effect of sin and readily accept as normal and OK many things God forbids. It's a trap!

Rock-N-Roll

It's so accepted to know the latest hit, to attend the greatest concerts, to wear the hottest T-shirt, and to own the latest stereo equipment both at home and in your wheels. "Got to be *bad!*"

It's a trap!

> ...whatever is true, whatever is honorable, whatever is right, whatever is pure, whatever is lovely, whatever is of good repute, if there is any excellence and if anything worthy of praise, let your mind dwell on these things.
>
> **Philippians 4:8 NAS**

Christian teenager, defend and stand up for the things of right-ness. Stand up for your Lord and for His Word. I am convinced if more Christian teens would defend the standard of righteousness as blatantly as they defend their rock-n-roll, we'd have thousands of devil bustin', God fearin', Jesus lovin', sin hatin', revival spreadin' youth groups from coast to coast! I see it coming! But it's going to require a daring faith that will stare the flesh in the face and declare, *"No more — in Jesus' Name!"*

FLESH TRAP #2: Dating

Hold on. I didn't say that dating is wrong or of the devil! God created you to like and be attracted to the opposite sex. You'd better be!

The problem happens when we follow the wrong pattern and apply the wrong examples. The problems arise when we build a relationship on the flesh, according to the world's standards, instead of following God's plan.

As a youth pastor of a large church for many years, I can tell you that Christian teens are not exempt from the temptations that arise from a fleshly relationship.

> Do not be deceived...Whatever a man sows, that he will also reap. For he who sows to his flesh will of the flesh reap corruption, but he who sows to the Spirit will of the Spirit reap everlasting life.
> Galatians 6:7,8 NKJ

Many times my wife Lisa and I have received phone calls from Christian teens who were in trouble.

They were either pregnant or got their girlfriend pregnant. It's a trap!

They didn't start the relationship with sex, but eventually, because the whole thing was founded in the flesh, passion gained a foothold and devastation was the result.

The flesh always wants more.

One thing you can count on concerning the flesh: *It always wants more!* It is never satisfied with just a little gratification. The flesh is a glutton!

A man told me how they trap monkeys in Africa. They have all kinds of traps. One of them is so simple you would not think it would ever catch anything, but it does. They take a big jar and put pieces of banana and other fruits and nuts on the bottom. When a monkey strolls along and looks inside, he is attracted to the fruit, so he reaches in and grabs a fistful of food. But because the opening of the jar is only big enough for the monkey to get its hand in, and not big enough to get a clenched fistful of food out, he is an easy catch. The monkey will not let go of that food, so while he struggles, a net is thrown over him, and he is trapped.

Sometimes our flesh acts the same way. Some people want satisfaction of their fleshly desires so much that they reach in that jar and hang on no matter what the preacher says, no matter what their parents say, no matter how much their heart is condemning them and trying to turn them to righteousness.

The flesh will not let go without a fight. All of a sudden, seemingly out of nowhere, the devil throws a net over your head, and you are trapped.

In an average dating situation this scene is very normal: school starts. A couple of weeks go by and one day, as you glance down the long hallway, you see her. There she is: "Wow, I'm in love." Finally you get the chance to meet her. Then, after a few days you get up the guts to ask her out. Nothing wrong so far. Everything seems to be going pretty good. Strictly friendship. You like each other. You have something in common...you both like the same pizza...you each like the way the other one looks. Even though you are a Christian, and assume she is one also, neither one has dedicated their dating life to the Lord up to this point. You are entering into a relationship the way everybody else has for years.

That evening, your palms begin to sweat, and you make the move. "Here I go, I'm gonna hold her hand!" Voila!

We're holding hands. But wait, *the flesh always wants more*. So your flesh says, "Let's graduate." It was fine holding hands, but now that's old. Suddenly, you're arm in arm. "Wow! What a sensation! I'm hers, she's mine. We're in love." After weeks of dating (possibly months) and getting more comfortable with each other, the flesh still screams for more. Kissing or more accurately known as "making out" has already found its way into the relationship. *The flesh always wants more*. If things continue the way they are going, soon this young man and young woman will become statistics.

As the heat begins to rise in this kind of relationship, the next step is petting. (And I'm not talking about petting your dog!) To explore, to feel, to indulge! These are some of the thoughts that flood the brain when temperatures rise. Clothes on, clothes off — petting is sin. Someone might say, "Oh, but it's just normal." Yes it is for a married couple. Outside of marriage, all sex is sin.

Have you ever said to yourself, "Hey, I'm in control here. I won't ever go beyond making out. No problem!" Famous last words.

I can't name one unmarried teenaged couple who engaged in pre-marital sex that *planned* to get the young woman pregnant. They were just expressing their love toward each other.

If you play with fire you are going to get burned. Check out the following scripture.

> Can a man take fire in his bosom, And his clothes not be burned?
>
> Or can a man walk on hot coals, And his feet not be scorched?
>
> So is the one who goes into his neighbor's wife or who has sex outside of marriage; Whoever touches her will not go unpunished.
>
> Proverbs 6:27-29 NAS

God said this. So even if you say, "I don't go all the way," remember *the flesh always wants more.* If you are engaged in a heated relationship and are making out, you have no guarantee that you will not go "all the way."

When you get to the point of heavy petting, obviously your spirit is not in control. Your flesh is in control, and it still isn't satisfied. You cannot stand on your will power alone. If you think you are going to hold on to your virginity with sheer will power alone, and you practice the heavy breathing routine in the car, on the couch, or wherever, with your girl/boyfriend, you are playing with fire. Remember, the flesh does not want to submit to the spirit.

> For the flesh sets its desire against the Spirit, and the Spirit against the flesh; for these are in opposition to one another, so that you may not do the things that you please.
>
> **Galatians 5:17 NAS**

When Jesus is not Lord over your sex life, your flesh is weaker than you think.

We've tried to dry many, many tears of young Christian and non-Christian ladies who thought they were strong enough to withstand, strong enough to say, "No." But they got burned.

Save your virginity for that special one God has chosen for you. It's worth the wait. You're only a virgin once. When it's gone, it's gone. There is no replacing it.

If You've Already Lost Your Virginity...

If you have already blown it, and you are filled with grief, hurt, shame, and condemnation, I want to tell you this: God still loves you very, very much. His forgiveness is waiting for you.

> If we confess our sins, he is faithful and just to forgive us our sin and to cleanse us from all unrighteousness.
>
> 1 John 1:9

Talk to the Lord. Express your feelings to Him. Receive your forgiveness and be cleansed from that unfortunate sin. Although you can never replace your virginity, God can create in you a wonderful love and expression for that special moment on your wedding night! He will restore and heal your emotions and your broken heart. Let Him do it right now.

Dedicate Your Dating Life to the Lord

Don't fall into the trap. Dedicate your dating life to the Lord. Be willing not to date for a season here and there. Be willing to obey God, obey your spirit, and say, "No," to the flesh. Avoid the world's example of dating! Eight times out of ten it will turn from liking to lusting which will always lead to a broken heart and a shattered relationship. God has something better planned for you!

FLESH TRAP #3: Lust

Lust is an "over-desire."

Lust is a strong desire to gratify the senses at any cost. If lust could talk, it probably would say something like this:

"Give me, give me, give me!

"Now, now, now!

"I don't want to wait,

"I can't hesitate.

"I hunger for fantasy and power."

In First John 2:16 NAS, we read what a world without God consists of:

> For all that is in the world, the lust of *the flesh* and the lust of *the eyes*, and the *boastful pride of life*....

People have gone to the extremes to gain fame, fortune, and power. Lust is the motivating factor.

As a teenager, the *lust of the flesh* and the *lust of the eyes* will approach you most every day in various shapes and sizes.

Fashion

Some people lust after the latest fad. To be (in style) and own the latest designer fashions is what they live for.

Look good. Dress sharp. Do the best you can with what you have. But *look out for the trap!* Sensual fashions are hot. In some crusades and churches where I have preached over the years, at times I have had to preach at the ceiling because of some of "the looseness" I observed in the audience.

If you have an overwhelming "over-desire" for the latest fads and fashions, check your heart. Don't be trapped by the self-centeredness this kind of thing breeds. Vanity runs rampant in the hearts of millions.

The Big "M"

We will not have a seminar on the big "M," but we will deal with it because of the staggering amount of bondage it brings upon hundreds of thousands of teens. "What is the big 'M'?" you may ask.

If you haven't already figured it out, we're talking about masturbation. Yup, this is a *major flesh trap*. Mainly because it is done in total privacy, in secret.

If people would be honest with themselves, many would come to the conclusion that they are actually hooked on the big "M." If they try to quit, they would find out they cannot (in their own ability).

The trap is in the mind. I believe there can be an innocent period (maybe the first time or two, God is the judge), when the big "M" is not sin. But the second lust controls the mind and becomes the motivation to do it, of course, then we know it is sin. Jesus said, ...**every one who** *looks on a woman to lust for her* **has committed adultery with her already** *in his heart* (Matt. 5:28 NAS).

Further bondage comes when condemnation shame and guilt take over. For men, the big "M" becomes a sin against their own manhood. For women, it is a sin against their own womanhood. The enemy would love to get you to hate yourself any way he can. The big "M" is a big trap!

FLESH TRAP #4: Rebellion

> **Children obey your parents in the Lord for this is right. Honor your father and mother which is the first commandment with a promise.**
>
> **Ephesians 6:1-2 NAS**

As elementary as this might sound, obeying your parents and honoring them while you are under their roof is a key to obtaining favor and prolonging your life. It is to your benefit that you obey good old Mom and Dad.

**That it may be *well with you,* and that
you may live long on the earth (Eph. 6:3
NAS).**

As unpopular as it may sound to
you, it is a wise thing to honor your
parent(s). As you do, God will honor
you. If you don't, you are opening yourself up for a rip-off! **If you are willing
and obedient, you shall eat the *good* of
the land; But if you refuse and *rebel,*
You shall *be devoured...* (Is. 1:19-20a
NKJ).**

As a teenager, my wife Lisa loved
Jesus Christ with all of her heart. But
her parents did not. Her dad was a
hard, hard man. He used to ground Lisa
from going to church for absolutely no
reason at all. The Spirit of God was
wooing him, and he tried to quench it
by stopping her. She would go to the
basement, get out her guitar, and worship and praise the Lord. One day in
fact, when she was grounded from
church, she received the baptism of the
Holy Spirit!

Instead of becoming bitter and rebellious, she chose to obey her parents. God honored her obedience. She actually fulfilled the scripture in First Timothy 4:12 that reads: ...**but rather in speech, conduct, love, faith and purity, show yourself an example of those who believe** (NAS). For years, she was one of the few examples her parents saw of a real Christian.

She was kicked out of her house, because she was going to marry a preacher (me). The persecution was that bad. Her dad told her, "I'm not going to walk you down the aisle. I'm not even going to show up for your wedding!"

She had to count the cost. At 18 years old, she had to make a decision. She moved out of her home and moved in with a couple from our church for a few months. During this time, we prayed and interceded. We prayed, "God, do a miracle."

My father-in-law ended up walking Lisa down the aisle. He was not even saved. He was born again a few years after our wedding, and two months after that, he was filled with the Holy Ghost in that same basement.

Her dad is now one of the most faithful intercessors in their church, and her mother has become solid in Christ.

One way God will teach teenagers some things in their lives is through their parents, whether or not the parents are saved. I exhort teenagers to obey their parents. God honors obedience!

Rebellion against daily priorities is a trap. Another word for this is "laziness." Ouch!

> **Poor is he who works with a negligent hand. But the hand of the diligent makes rich.**
> **Proverbs 10:4 NAS**

> **The soul of the sluggard craves and gets nothing. But the soul of the diligent is made fat.**
> **Proverbs 13:4 NAS**

Daily priorities include:

a) rest. You should have no problem with that one, but don't over do it. Too much sleep and rest will make you feel gross!

b) exercise. Your body needs it. Take some time to get your heart pumping every day.

c) time in the Word of God. **I have not departed from the command of His lips; I have treasured the words of His mouth more than my necessary food** (Job 23:12 NAS).

Man shall not live on bread alone, but on every word that proceeds out of the mouth of God (Matt. 4:4 NAS). Spending some time each day in the Word of God is *necessary* to whip the flesh. It is not only necessary, it is demanded if you really want to be a winner!

d) time in prayer. Jesus was a man of prayer. He is our example. **With all prayer and petition pray at all times in the Spirit...be on the alert...** (Eph. 6:18 NAS).

Prayer is communication and nourishment. It brings a refreshing. Prayer is a shield; it releases boldness, and breeds spiritual liberty. *Prayer is the lifeline of all believers. It is where we receive orders from headquarters.*

All four of these things are essential and necessary for you to experience a successful day. When these priorities are ignored on a daily basis, there will arise a heaviness in your spirit telling you that something is *out of focus.*

Are you starting to feel like a warrior yet? You can overcome the flesh and give first place to the Spirit! You can do it! God believes in you — He's made you to soar with the eagles, not crawl with the worms! You've got winning stuff on the inside of you! It's always too soon to quit!

FLESH TRAP #5: Unwholesome Associates (Friends)

> **Do not be deceived: "bad company corrupts good morals."**
> **1 Corinthians 15:33 NAS**

This is a big one!

How many times have you heard of someone *turning bad* because they began to hang out with a "bad" crowd? The list is endless.

As a Christian teenager, God has called you to intimately associate with those of like faith. (See 2 Cor. 6:14-18.) He wants you to hang around those who will build you up, not tear you down. He wants you to fellowship with those who can minister to you and pray for you when you are down. He wants the best for you.

This does not mean that you totally avoid and treat others like dirt. No! You are to be a light to them and bring them into the good life. (See 1 Pet. 2:9.)

As you surround yourself with godly friends, you will become more godly. **He who walks with wise men will be wise, But the companion of fools will suffer harm** (Prov. 13:20 NAS).

But if you surround yourself with ungodly people, the reverse will occur.

The "In-Crowd" isn't always in!

Look out — it can be a trap!

FLESH TRAP #6: Flirting With the Forbidden

There shall not be found among you anyone who makes his son or daughter pass through the fire, one who uses divination, one who practices witchcraft, or who interprets omens, or a sorcerer,

Or one who casts a spell, or a medium, or a spiritist, or one who calls up the dead.

For whoever does these things is detestable to the Lord....
Deuteronomy 18:10-12 NAS

Flirting with the forbidden has become ultra popular and is increasing in popularity as we approach the sound of the trumpet.

However popular and accepted it might be in your neighborhood, school,

clique, or community, this is one trap that has one of the most devastating consequences. Ultimately, every realm involving the slightest occult practice will eventually end up denying the Christ and blaspheming the Holy Spirit.

Interestingly enough, the forbidden is listed in Galatians 5 as a work of the flesh. Just as any other work of the flesh, the initial desire and interest to explore this area comes from our *own lust* as described in James, chapter one. But just as the others, if meditated upon and practiced long enough, along comes the trapper, which is the devil or one of his demons.

Cold Hearts = Hot Flesh

Any one or more of these areas can produce a cold, calloused heart if we fall into the trap.

If you have ever played guitar, you know what a callous is. When you first learn to play guitar, your fingers get sore after only 10 or 15 minutes. The more you play, the more calloused they get, until you get to a point where they never hurt.

A callous is beneficial on the end of your fingers. Spiritually speaking, though, a callous is not beneficial. When we stop reading the Bible and praying, sooner or later, the world's system becomes more appealing. The result is a cold, calloused heart. Once your heart becomes cold, the flesh becomes very hot. Cold heart equals hot flesh.

There is no middle of the road when you allow your carnal mind to call the shots. Eventually, it will catch up with you, and you will develop a calloused, insensitive heart. Your heart will get colder by the day, colder by the week, colder by the month, and your flesh will get hotter, hotter, and hotter.

But the cycle can reverse itself. God wants your spirit hot. He said to the Laodiceans in the book of Revelation that He would rather they be cold or hot. That means that He does not want lukewarm Christians. (Rev. 3:15,16.)

God is not a lukewarm God. That is why you need to make up your mind that you are going to follow God and not your flesh.

When the Holy Spirit says, *"No!"* inside you and you go ahead and do it anyway, then your heart becomes colder and colder.

God Honors Obedience

Not doing what God tells you to do is one way of rejecting God's direction for your life.

Your heart gets calloused and cold when you continually reject the divine direction. When you feel the conviction of the Holy Spirit rise up in your life, and you know you should repent and turn from sin and ask God's forgiveness, *DO IT!* The calloused person will push that voice away, and pretty soon the voice of the Spirit will become weaker and weaker.

> **Today if you hear His voice,
> do not harden your hearts...**
> **Hebrews 3:7-8a NAS**

No matter how *fleshed-out* you have become, there is always a way *in* to the Father's arms, and there is always an escape hatch *out* from the snare of the fowler!

5
Dealing With the Feelings

For we walk by faith, not by sight.

2 Corinthians 5:7

Let me tell you a story about a lady.

One day an evangelist came to the lady's town. He had a great revival meeting going, and at the end of one of his meetings, the altars were filled with people. This elderly lady at the end of the altar wept convulsively, crying so loudly and making so much noise that she distracted the people. So the evangelist made his way down to her and said, "Ma'am, what is it? What may I pray with you about?"

She looked up at him with those sad, waterfilled eyes and said, "Preacher, I'd like you to pray that the devil will stop tempting me the rest of my life. He just always gives me all kinds of trouble. Will you pray for me?"

He said, "Sure will, ma'am." He grabbed her by the hand and said, "Let's pray that you die right now."

Wiping her tears, she looked at him and said, "What do you mean? I don't have many years left as it is."

He went on to explain. "Well, ma'am, what I mean to say to you is that as long as you're in this life, living in that body, you're going to have to learn how to contend with the devil. You're going to have to learn how to fight the temptations of the flesh, or lie down and die."

Sometimes we are like that elderly lady. We say, "God, deliver me from my flesh." But the only way you can be delivered from your flesh is if you go home to be with the Lord.

"But you just don't understand how hard it is," you might say. "These feelings are real! Sometimes I am overwhelmed by emotion and can't seem to pull away from it all!"

The good news in the face of all this is: *You do not have to let your feelings rule you!* But you do have to deal with what you feel!

No matter how great the temptation is and how you may feel, remember this: *The devil or the flesh can never make you do anything!* They cannot lay you flat on your back, tie you to a bed, and pour a fifth of vodka down your throat to make you get drunk.

The only *in* they have is when you give them permission by believing the lie of deception and of your feelings. When you say, "OK, I think I'll do it," it is at that point when the flesh takes over and leads you places where you shouldn't be, speaks things through your lips, things that you shouldn't say, and proceeds to oppose the Spirit in any way.

But before the flesh and the enemy can begin this process of sin,

they must first get their foot in. This is where your feelings come in.

You Can't Always Trust Your Feelings!

"Luke, trust your feelings." Remember that famous line in the blockbuster hit, *Star Wars*? As believers, until our minds are renewed by the Word of God, we cannot totally trust our senses in every given situation.

> And I, brethren, could not speak to you as to spiritual men, but as to men of flesh, as to babes in Christ. I gave you milk to drink, not solid food; for you were not yet able to receive it. Indeed, even now you are not yet able, for you are still fleshly.
>
> 1 Corinthians 3:1-3a NAS

These guys were still men of the flesh — fleshly or carnal. Another word for carnal is *sense ruled.* That simply means that carnal, fleshly people are led by their feelings and not by the Spirit.

One mark of a true disciple of Jesus Christ is the denial of rulership. A true disciple has denied the right to rulership. (See Luke 9:23.) A sense-ruled person is constantly doing whatever *he* wishes without acknowledging the Lord or anyone else. As unfortunate as it is, it still remains true that even many Christians do their own thing without consulting the Lord.

> **Trust in the Lord with all your heart** (walk by faith), **And do not lean on your own understanding** (feelings, reason, or emotions). **In all your ways acknowledge Him, and He will make your paths straight.**
>
> Proverbs 3:5-6 NAS (with author's paraphrase.)

Recognize the fact that your feelings can deceive you. Check them out. When a situation arises and you feel tempted to follow your senses, stop for a moment and ask yourself if what you are feeling is in harmony with the Word of God and a Christlike lifestyle. Jesus said, **My sheep know my voice and the voice of a stranger they will *not* follow** (paraphrase John 10:4,5 NAS). Pause for a moment in the midst of that temptation and listen to your spirit! What is he saying?

You can bet your left shoe that He is speaking. Now the question is: Do you really want to hear, trust, and obey that still small voice?

Back to the dating scene for a moment. When you are with your date and the heat starts to rise, your feelings go crazy! Passion wants control. Your hormones are on overload. What are you going to do? Follow your flesh? Or listen to your spirit? *There is always a choice to make. God would never leave you stranded without a way of escape!*

In each and every tempting situation, there is *always, always* a right road to take. But you must always take the first step on that right road of escape *by faith* believing with all your heart that God will not let you down.

God said, **I will never leave you *nor forsake you*** (Heb. 13:5 NKJ). *The Amplified Bible* translates this verse as **[...I will] not in any degree leave you helpless, nor forsake, nor let [you] down.** *The American Standard Version* says, **...I will in no wise fail thee....**

Many people have allowed their feelings to become mountains because they have not had the desire or taken the time to look for the escape hatch. Because you are into this book this far, I am assuming that you desire to find that hatch. The promises that God has made to those who endure (resist) the temptations of the flesh are dynamite! Here's one that'll get you going:

> **Blessed is a man who perse-
> veres under trial; for once he has
> been approved, he will receive the
> crown of life, which the Lord has
> promised to those who love Him.**
> **James 1:12 NAS**

Challenge Those Wrong Feelings!

Deal with what you feel! Just don't be a wimp about it and sit back and do nothing. Never accept feelings as fact all the time. Feelings are only fact when they line up with the Word of Truth! God's Word is fact! It is the ultimate authority! God's Word *is unequivocal, indisputable truth!*

If you were set free from hating your mom or dad, and you completely forgave them for any ill will or wrong they committed toward you, then you understand what it feels like to be released from that kind of bondage. Some feelings are good. Hey, don't forget Who put your senses in you! God did, and He has a purpose for them!

But let's imagine for a moment that something took place between you and your parents which brought the thought into your mind, "See, you still hate them, you were never set free from that. If you were, then why are you feeling this way?" That feeling and thought *is a lie!* Just because a thought enters your mind does not mean that you have to accept it!

Now deal with that feeling! Locate the escape hatch, and don't ever be trapped by that lie again. Jesus said, **If you abide in My Word, then you are truly disciples of Mine; and you shall know the truth, and the *truth shall make you free.* (John 8:31,32 NAS).

The truth is that you were set free from hatred. Now Satan, through the flesh, is trying to steal that truth, destroy your faith, and kill your relationship with your parents! (See John 10:10.)

6

Locating the Escape Hatch

> No temptation has overtaken you but such as is common to man; and God is faithful, who will not allow you to be tempted beyond what you are able, *but with the temptation will provide the way of escape* also, that you may be able to endure it.
>
> **1 Corinthians 10:13 NAS**

The door to the escape hatch from the temptations of the flesh is found in the mighty name of Jesus and in His Word!

When Jesus was tempted by the devil in the wilderness (Luke 4:1-14), He did something which led to total victory over the temptations every time — Jesus spoke the Word of God against the opposing force.

After each temptation, Jesus started each resisting statement with the words, "It is written..." then He continued to quote scripture to finish it.

> ...and they overcame him
> by the blood of the Lamb, and by
> *the word* of their testimony...
>> **Revelation 12:11**

It is the Word believed in your heart and spoken out of your mouth against your foes that will bring freedom! This Word is more than just mere words. In the face of opposition, this Word of Faith is an unbeatable force. The flesh and the devil are no match for it.

When the Flesh Rises Up, Temptation Comes

Here is what to do when temptation comes on the scene:

1. Remind it that it no longer rules!

Tell the flesh that you (the spirit or new man) are now calling the shots and that you will not go along with it any longer. (Eph. 4: 22-24.)

2. Resist it by speaking the Word.

Out of your mouth, no matter where you are (at school, in a restaurant, at home), resist the temptation by speaking the Word of God. Begin to memorize scriptures that will help you resist. God has a scripture for every situation!

3. Don't let up until either the temptation departs, the desire to flesh out leaves, or Jesus comes via the rapture! In other words, stay with it until you win!

Hey, dude, this stuff works if we will dare to work it! It's not over till it's over, and it's not over until you and Jesus win! This should be your attitude.

4. When needed, get out of the place that is contributing to the temptation. Flee! Remember what Paul told Timothy? "Flee youthful lusts." If that means to physically get out of a place that feeds your flesh and temptation,

then do it! Once again I remind you that *you must want to*!

When a tornado rises up, people begin to run for shelter. Sometimes the storm gets so nasty that it blows dust, debris, and rain so thick that it gets difficult to see clearly to find the shelter.

Sometimes the flesh can rise up with such an intensity that it blows up all kinds of dust to the point that it gets hard to see clearly to find the escape hatch.

But you know what? Those who want to live badly enough will find that shelter! They will recall in their minds where the path is even though they cannot see it very clearly.

If you want freedom from the flesh badly enough, you'll not quit looking for the hatch just because the wind blows up some dust in your face! If it really doesn't matter either way, then you will eventually reap what you've sown.

For those who are according to the flesh set their minds on the things of the flesh, but those who are according to the Spirit, the things of the Spirit.

For the mind set on the flesh is death, but the mind set on the Spirit is life and peace.

Romans 8:5,6 NAS

Set your mind on the Spirit and reap life and peace. The other mind set will kill you.

There is safety in the shelter behind the hatch!

He who dwells in the *shelter of the Most High* Will abide in the shadow of the Almighty.

I will say to the Lord, "My refuge and my fortress, My God, in whom I trust!"

For it is He *who delivers you from the snare of the trapper*, And from the deadly pestilence.

He will cover you with His pinions, And under His wings you may seek refuge...."

Psalm 91:1-4 NAS

God has not left you alone. He is a loving, caring, and compassionate Lord. He has provided the way of escape for those who will seek it and do it. You've got winning stuff on the inside of you and you can do it!

7

Breaking Bad Habits

Every one of us has habits; habits do not always have to be bad. Have you ever put your left shoe on first? ...turned the shower on before or after you got in?...eaten a good meal every day?...gone to church on Sunday?

Most of us do not remember these types of things. They have become automatic. They are habits — good habits!

Yet, there are other things that we do over and over again, that are harmful to us and displeasing to God. These are *bad habits*.

A bad habit is any thought or action that becomes involuntary or compulsive through regular repetition and is opposed to the teaching of the Word of God. Needless to say, God wants us to get rid of these habits that displease Him.

What Causes a Bad Habit

A bad or harmful habit is caused by repeatedly giving in to the impulses of the flesh. Bad habits used to be temptations that we would resist from time to time, and give in to from time to time.

> Don't you realize that you can choose your own master? You can choose sin (with death) or else obedience (with acquittal). The one to whom you offer yourself — he will take you and be your master and you will be his slave.
>
> Romans 6:16 TLB

Bad habits spring out of our flesh. By giving in to a sin time and again, sooner or later it will become regular —it will become a habit which will bring bondage. This bondage fulfills the enemy's desire to discourage and defeat each Christian by establishing us in activities that do not please God.

Steps to Breaking a Bad Habit

1. We must be serious about quitting.

No one breaks a bad habit unless he really wants to. It is easy to observe our bad habits and fool ourselves into thinking that our enslaving practices are not that damaging. That type of reasoning comes only from the flesh that does not want to let go and that *resists any kind of positive change.*

Bad habits are serious because:

a) God thinks they are serious.

And if your right eye makes you stumble, tear it out, and throw it from you; for it is better for you that one of the parts of your body perish, than for your whole body to be thrown into hell.

And if your right hand makes you stumble, cut if off, and throw it from you; for it is better for you that one of the parts of your body perish, than for your whole body to go into hell.

Matthew 5:29,30 NAS

b) They have already held us back from fulfilling our potential for God.

Therefore, if a man cleanses himself from these things, he will be a vessel for honor, sanctified, useful to the master, prepared for every good work.

2 Timothy 2:21 NAS

c) They will lead to trouble in the future.

Do not be deceived, God is not mocked; for whatever a man sows, this he will also reap. For the one who sows to his own flesh shall from the flesh reap correction, but the one who sows to the Spirit shall from the Spirit reap eternal life.

Galatians 6:7,8 NAS

2. We must know what we are going to do about the bad habits.

There must be *an act of our wills* and *a commitment to God*. Some think they can still enjoy their habit and maintain a rich and peaceful Christian life. That is referred to in James 1:8 (NAS) as **a double-minded man... unstable in all his ways.** A double-minded man is undecided between two choices.

Sometimes he chooses God's ways and other times the ways of the flesh.

Because of his indecision he is unpredictable and untrustworthy as far as God is concerned. His life is a series of ups and downs, victories and defeats, joys and frustrations. God does not want us to be flaky in our commitment to follow Him. He wants us to have one mind and follow wholeheartedly, whatever our plan of action might be. Double-minded thinking is fruitless.

> No servant can serve two masters; for either he will hate the one, and love the other, or else he will hold to one, and despise the other. You cannot serve God and mammon.
>
> Luke 16:13 NAS

It is God's will that we decide who we will obey and then commit ourselves totally to follow that master with our whole being.

In the New Testament there was a church that couldn't decide whether to follow God or their flesh. So they tried a little of both. Jesus said, **I know your** deeds, that you are neither hot nor cold; I would that you were cold or hot. So because you are lukewarm, and neither hot nor cold, I will spit you out of My mouth (Rev. 3:15,16 NAS).

God wants His followers to have a will that is determined to obey Him no matter what the feelings or circumstances might be.

Can you say, "I am determined to serve God because of His greatness, no matter what my feelings say to oppose me?"

3. We must know that we can win.

To break a bad habit, we must know that in God's power, we do not have to continue practicing destructive habits!

Many people have just about given up in their struggle against sin. They think the flesh is some kind of evil taskmaster over whom they have no power. So they rationalize their bad, sinful habits as though there is nothing they can do to quit.

God wants to encourage you to know not only that victory over the old sin nature is possible, but also that we are in fact, through faith in Christ, dead to its impulses to do wrong!

Because of the death and resurrection of Jesus Christ, that old man of sin has died, therefore, it has no power to make us perform sinful habits.

Of course not! Should we keep on sinning when we don't have to? For sin's power over us was broken when we became Christians and were baptized to become a part of Jesus Christ; through his death the power of your sinful nature was shattered.

Your old evil desires were nailed to the cross with him; that part of you that loves to sin was crushed and fatally wounded, so that your sin-loving body is no longer under sin's control, no longer needs to be a slave to sin; for when you are deadened to sin you are freed from all its allure and its power over you.

Romans 6:2,3,6,7 TLB

But we might ask:

- If my sin nature has been crushed and if it is powerless to control my life...

- If my old desires were nailed to the cross, and if that part of me that wants to sin was fatally wounded...

Why then am I so driven by these crazy, sinful desires that are supposed to be dead?

The flesh cannot make us perform bad habits when we live by faith, believing that we are dead to its power. Saturate yourself in the Word of Faith! When you do, this truth will become a reality to you.

4. Draw near to God, and apply the power of the Holy Spirit. (James 4:8,9.) ...**But be filled with the Spirit** (Eph. 5:18b). God must fill your heart and mind at a time like this.

5. Realize that natural weapons cannot win spiritual battles.

We, in ourselves, are no match for Satan or our flesh. They are much too deceitful and powerful. But with Jesus Christ in us we have tremendous authority to resist Satan's bondage and *force him to leave!*

> **For though we walk in the flesh, we do not war according to the flesh.**
>
> **For the weapons of our warfare are not carnal but mighty in God for pulling down strongholds.**
>
> **2 Corinthians 10:3,4 NKJ**

That bad habit has become a stronghold in your life. The weapons we possess in Christ, which are not made of or from the flesh, but of and from the Spirit, have the ability to destroy that stronghold! **You are from God, little children, and have overcome them; because greater is He who is in you than he who is in the world** (1 John 4:4 NAS).

Will power alone will never bring total victory. But Spirit power will! Use the name of Jesus against that stronghold. Name the bad habit by name. God has given Jesus *the name above every name.* (Phil. 2:9.) That habit is below the Name! Proclaim it! Demand it! In Jesus' name.

6. Claim the Blood of Jesus Christ.

Devils tremble at the Blood of Jesus! They can never forget the great work accomplished at Calvary on the cross. Claim the Blood of Jesus. (See Rev. 12:11.)

7. Pray!

Here is a prayer that you can make your very own as you go before the Father to start ridding yourself of this habit. Let it be personal. Let it come from your heart. Let it set you free!

Dear Heavenly Father, I thank you that I can draw near to You. I thank You that I can now be filled with Your Holy Spirit. By faith I believe this.

I realize that I can do nothing by myself, so I am claiming the authority You have given me in Your Son Jesus Christ who lives inside of me. I am claiming Your promise that the blood of Jesus can give me power over sin. Father, in the name of Jesus by the power of His blood, I resist the work of the devil and the flesh in my life, and I command this (these) bad habit(s) of _____ to flee my life!

Greater is He that is in me than he that is in the world. So by faith I believe that You, Father, are allowing me to resist this temptation, and it is taking effect in me now. In Jesus' name, Amen.

8

Preventive Medicine

Walk in the Spirit, and you shall not fulfill the lust of the flesh.

Galatians 5:16 NKJ

To prevent something bad or worse from happening to their patients, doctors of all practices prescribe preventive medicine. It could be a prescription from a drugstore or a simple directive to avoid certain strenuous activities that may be dangerous to the patients' health in the future.

With this in mind, Galatians 5:16 is a type of preventive medicine to assist the believer in avoiding unnecessary flesh traps. If we apply this medication of the Spirit we will find ourselves living happier, more fulfilled lives with not as many distractions from the flesh.

Learn the Walk of the Spirit

To walk in the Spirit is to let your steps be guided and directed by the Holy Spirit.

> In *all your ways* acknowledge Him, *And He shall direct your paths.*
>
> **Proverbs 3:6 NKJ**

To walk in the Spirit is to know the voice of the Lord and of your spirit. Your spirit has a voice. Some call it their conscience. It is the real you trying to get God's message through to help you in all aspects of your life. How do you get to know that still small voice of your spirit? By listening.

We get so busy sometimes that we do not listen to the most important voice in our lives. There is so much clutter. Why is it that a child can recognize his mother's voice so readily in any given situation? Because that child has been with Mom. Mom has been with the child for years. They have gotten to know each other's voice tones, expressions, and other characteristics. In the same way, as you spend time with the Lord in His Word and in prayer, you will begin to learn His voice tones, expressions, and other characteristics. You will learn the same concerning the voice of your inner man, your spirit.

To help you avoid future flesh traps, listed below are some *preventive tips*. As you find those which relate to your life, begin applying them with trust that they will help you be a stronger Christian. Receive these tips as a word of wisdom for the benefit of your future.

TIP #1: Run from or resist the circumstances that may tempt you to sin.

Each one of us has weak spots in our lives. We all have areas that we are more vulnerable in than other areas. Almost every temptation of the flesh has a circumstance or an object that allows the process of temptation to start and continue.

In many cases, if these circumstances or objects were not accessible, available, to the person, the temptation would either disappear or never even start. For example, if a person with a drinking problem or smoking problem could no longer get to the booze or the tobacco, the problem would begin to disappear. If someone with a habit of wasting time watching TV gave his TV away, he would eliminate the source of the problem.

To stay away from circumstances or objects that feed our flesh, God expects us to do the best we can with what we know. Romans 13:14 says:

> **But put on the Lord Jesus Christ, and** *make no provision for the flesh* **in regard to its lust.** (NAS)

> **But ask the Lord Jesus Christ to help you live as you should,** *and don't make plans to enjoy evil.* (TLB)

In the book of Proverbs, King Solomon was instructing his son about immoral, godless women. He said:

> **Now then, my sons, listen to me, And do not depart from the**

> words of my mouth. Keep your
> way far from her, And do not go
> near the door of her house, Lest
> you give your vigor to others, And
> your years to the cruel one.
>
> Proverbs 5:7-9 NAS

King Solomon knew his sons could plan their lives so that they could avoid becoming involved with rowdy women.

Sometimes Satan and his demons arrange for us to come upon objects and/or circumstances that lead to sin. When this happens, God's command for us is *to flee, to get out of there!* (See 2 Tim. 2:22.)

TIP #2: Stay busy for God.

I heard a great man of God preaching at a large crusade years ago. He said something that night that was to become a standard in my life forever. He said, "Stay busy for God. It will keep you out of trouble, and make you a servant. When God wants to use you, He'll know where to look, because God uses people who are busy doing Kingdom work."

Of course, we do not need to be workaholics, but we do need to maintain vision in our lives. My grandma used to tell me that an idle mind is the devil's workshop. I thought she was just nagging me. How true that is. When we are bored and have nothing to do, especially teenagers, temptation becomes a greater risk.

a) Get involved in your church's youth program. Become a leader, be a servant, offer your talents and abilities to your pastor and youth director.

b) Get a job in the summer.

c) Go on a missions trip.

It requires concentration and work to raise the money, and the result of a well-planned missions trip will change your life.

d) Begin a wholesome hobby that will not take away from your time with God or your family time. Find something that interests you and that you enjoy.

TIP #3: Keep godly company.

Remember First Corinthians 15:33:

Do not be deceived: "Bad company corrupts good morals" (NAS).

Maintaining healthy friendships is one of the most important preventive tips. Because we are so influenced by our friends, eventually we will begin acting like they do. Iron sharpens iron. (Prov. 27:17.) Good friends who believe like you do will promote Godly principles and standards. Therefore, you will not find yourself in tempting situations so often because you are with people who do not encourage evil.

He who walks with wise men will be wise, But the companion of fools will suffer harm.
Proverbs 13: 20 NAS

TIP #4: Develop a regular (daily) prayer and study time.

> **Blessed is the man Who walks not in the counsel of the ungodly, Nor stands in the path of sinners, nor sits in the seat of the scornful:** *but his delight is in the law of the Lord, And in His law he does meditate, day and night.*
>
> **Psalm 1:1-3 NKJ**

Spending time in God's Word at the start of each day and taking time to fellowship with the Heavenly Father in prayer is *the most important preventive tip.*

If you have never disciplined yourself in this daily practice, it may be tough getting started. Remember, your flesh wants to keep things like they were — lazy and loose. The devil will stop at nothing to create distractions to discourage you from getting started. Satan knows that once you start plugging in to God, you will become a threat to his plan upon the earth, and he will have a more difficult time deceiving you into fleshly bondage.

The Word of God creates a protective covering around and about you. (See Ps. 91.) The Word of God is the sword of the Spirit which becomes your weapon against all evil when it is in your heart, then spoken out of your mouth with bold faith. (See Eph. 6:17.)

God has given you weapons — use them!

God has granted you wisdom — apply it!

God has given you life — love it!

God has given you Jesus — know Him!

9

Conclusion

I urge you therefore, brethren, by the mercies of God, to present your bodies a living and holy sacrifice, acceptable to God, which is your spiritual service of worship.

And do not be conformed to this world, but be transformed by the renewing of your mind, that you may prove what the will of God is, that which is good and acceptable and perfect.

Romans 12:1,2 NAS

The battle between Spirit and flesh is very real. But so is the victory! Present your bodies to God as a living sacrifice. Realize that you are not your own; therefore, you should glorify God in your body and spirit which are His.

As you do, you will never regret it! The things that you sacrifice now will pay off in a little while. We are not always going to have to mess with the flesh.

Now I say this, brethren, that flesh and blood cannot inherit the kingdom of God; nor does the perishable inherit the imperishable.

Behold, I tell you a mystery; we shall not all sleep, but we shall all be changed, in a moment, in the twinkling of an eye, at the last trumpet; for the trumpet will sound, and the dead will be raised imperishable, and we shall be changed.

For this perishable must put on the imperishable, and this mortal must put on immortality. But when this perishable will have put on the imperishable, and this mortal will have put on immortality, then will come about the saying that is written, "DEATH IS SWALLOWED UP IN VICTORY.

O DEATH, WHERE IS YOUR VICTORY? O DEATH, WHERE IS YOUR STING?" The sting of death is sin, and the power of sin is the law; but thanks be to

God, who gives us the victory through our Lord Jesus Christ. Therefore, my beloved brethren, be steadfast, immovable, always abounding in the work of the Lord, knowing that your toil is not in vain in the Lord.

1 Corinthians 15:50-58 NAS

One day soon, when we go home to forever be with the Lord, this flesh will be changed into immortality! This flesh is only temporal. Lift up your head! Keep your eyes on Jesus and remind yourself day by day that serving the Lord and resisting evil is always worth it!

So the next time your flesh rises up, remind it that it is no longer in control! Just say, *"Hey, Flesh, move over! This is the spirit talking to you!"*

References

Scripture quotations marked (NAS) are taken from the *New American Standard Bible*, © The Lockman Foundation, 1960, 1962, 1968, 1971, 1973, 1975, 1977, and used by permission.

Scripture quotations marked (TLB) are from *The Living Bible*, © 1971 by Tyndale House Publishers, Wheaton, Illinois. Used by permission.

Scripture quotations marked (AMP) are from the *Amplified New Testament*, © 1954, 1958, 1987, by the Lockman Foundation, and are used by permission.

Scripture quotations marked (ASV) are from the *American Standard Version*, published by Thomas Nelson & Sons and International Council of Religious Education, and used by permission.

Scripture quotations marked (NKJ) are from the *New King James Version*, © 1979, 1982 by Thomas Nelson, Inc. Used by permission.